WHOHQ

The Who Was?
Activity Book

Puzzles, mazes, and tons of fun based on the
New York Times Best-Selling Who Was? series

by Jordan London
illustrations by Nancy Harrison
with additional art by Scott Burroughs

Penguin Workshop
An Imprint of Penguin Random House

PENGUIN WORKSHOP
Penguin Young Readers Group
An Imprint of Penguin Random House LLC

Frame art (pages 41, 59, 71): Nataliashein/Thinkstock

ISBN 9781524789978   10 9 8 7 6 5 4 3 2 1

Welcome to the wonderful world of Who Was?, full of historical facts, famous folks, and even horses! (We're talking to you, Seabiscuit!) This book is filled with activities, games, and stickers for future famous people, just like *you*!

Are you a musician? An artist? A sports legend in the making? A budding film director? A future president or astronaut? There are many paths to making it into the history books. Turn the page to help discover your own!

Answer Key begins on page 92.

Great Authors

Answer the questions, and test your knowledge of some of the greatest authors in history.

Across

5. The most famous author of the Victorian era. He is known for such classics as *Great Expectations* and *A Christmas Carol*.

8. A fighter pilot in World War II who wrote about a boy flying across the sky in a giant peach

9. A woman who grew up in a little house on the prairie

Down

1. One of the greatest playwrights in history. He is best known for writing about star-crossed young love, something rotten in Denmark, and how to tame a shrew.

2. An author who also illustrated his picture books. He wrote about the wild rumpus.

3. An American author who wrote about a young boy named Huckleberry Finn

4. She created the magical wizarding world of a boy named Harry.

6. An American author known for his poems and scary stories about a raven and the tell-tale heart

7. Once voted "least likely to succeed" in college, this author became famous for his silly rhymes, his even sillier drawings, and the occasional green eggs and ham.

Crossword (filled in):

- 1 Down: William Shakespeare
- 2 Down: Maurice Sendak
- 3 Down: Mark Twain
- 4 Down: J. K. Rowling
- 5 Across: Charles Dickens
- 6 Down: Edgar Allan Poe
- 7 Down: Dr. Seuss
- 8 Across: Roald Dahl
- 9 Across: Laura Ingalls Wilder

Word bank:

Charles Dickens ✓	Mark Twain 9
Dr. Seuss ✓	Maurice Sendak ✓
Edgar Allan Poe	Roald Dahl 9
J. K. Rowling 9	William Shakespeare
Laura Ingalls Wilder 8	

14

13

5

Wave Your Own Flag!

During the Revolutionary War, Betsy Ross was a seamstress who made blankets and tents for the American army. Some historians believe that she was responsible for sewing the first American flag.

Use the space below to create a flag for your own country!

Connect the Dots:
The Peacekeepers

Mother Teresa lived among very poor people in Calcutta, India, and her life's mission was to help the sick and dying. She received the Nobel Peace Prize in 1979.

Mother Teresa

In 1920, **Gandhi** became the leader of the Indian National Congress, a strong political voice for the people of India. He was put in prison for encouraging other people to break British laws that were unfair to the people of India. Noncooperation and nonviolence were his greatest weapons against the unfair treatment of the Indian population.

Gandhi

Connect the dots to reveal a symbol of peace.

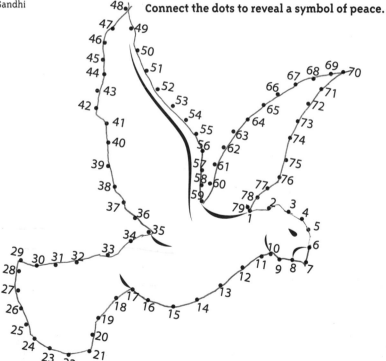

Historical Hair

Have you noticed that some well-known people have amazingly famous hair? Let's take a look at some historically famous hairdos.

Dolly Parton is known for her big hair and big voice! Growing up in Tennessee, Dolly dreamed of becoming a country-music superstar, and she did! She has written many hit songs, including "I Will Always Love You."

Marie Antoinette was known for her sky-high wigs. Born into royalty in 1755, she married the future king of France at age fourteen and became queen by age eighteen. In addition to her hair, she was known for her extravagant lifestyle, which ultimately led to her losing her head during the French Revolution.

Albert Einstein may have been called a "lazy dog" by one of his teachers, but he grew up to be a brilliant physicist who would occasionally forget to brush his hair, resulting in his wild 'do!

Andy Warhol went bald in his twenties, but he wouldn't let that stop him from expressing himself through his hair. He wore fantastic wigs throughout his life.

Draw your own new hairstyles on the famous heads below.
Maybe your hair will be historical someday, too!

God Save the Queen!

While she was a teenager in the sixteenth century, Elizabeth was imprisoned in the Tower of London for two months. Learn more about Queen Elizabeth I below, and help her escape the tower in the maze on the next page!

Fact: Queen Elizabeth I was a great fan and supporter of William Shakespeare and his plays.

Fact: As queen, Elizabeth knighted Sir Francis Drake, an explorer who sailed around the world.

Fact: Elizabeth owned hundreds of dresses. She destroyed any portraits of herself that she did not approve of.

Fact: Queen Elizabeth I's father started his own church, the Church of England.

MY MOTTO IN LATIN WAS *SEMPER EADEM*, WHICH MEANS "ALWAYS THE SAME."

START!

Fact: Elizabeth was crowned queen in 1558, when she was twenty-five years old!

FINISH!

Match the Frontier Facts

Davy Crockett and Daniel Boone are two legendary American frontiersmen who are frequently confused for each other. In fact, Daniel Boone was fifty-two years older than Davy Crockett. Test your knowledge of both men below. Draw a line between each fact and its matching frontiersman.

- I was born near what is now Birdsboro, Pennsylvania.

- I was born near what is now Limestone, Tennessee.

- I was known for my coonskin cap.

- I was held captive by American Indians from the Shawnee tribe because I was hunting on their lands.

- I was elected to Congress in 1827.

- As a teenager, I killed my first bear when I should have been tending my family's cows.

- I claimed to have killed 105 bears in one season.

- I rescued my thirteen-year-old daughter, Jemima, when she was kidnapped by American Indians.

- I led the first pioneers across the Appalachian Mountains.

- I fought and died at the Alamo.

Daniel Boone

Davy Crockett

The French Chef

Julia Child brought French cooking to America in the 1960s with her television show *The French Chef*. While living in France following World War II, Julia discovered her love of French food and soon enrolled in culinary school. She went on to write *Mastering the Art of French Cooking*. Her humorous and honest approach to food changed the course of cooking in America.

Master these cooking terms, and then find them in the word search below.

H	S	I	N	R	A	G	A	R	M	E	H
A	A	V	F	O	G	G	R	R	E	F	A
D	U	Q	I	A	Z	O	O	L	B	W	B
B	T	Y	J	S	U	K	A	M	R	Q	R
S	E	W	D	X	J	V	S	A	Z	Y	O
E	K	I	I	M	P	I	T	Q	O	B	I
A	C	V	C	Y	E	N	G	R	I	L	L
R	X	Z	E	T	H	U	N	A	Y	T	M
S	A	H	G	P	A	R	E	B	J	W	G

Broil: To cook food directly *under* a very hot heat source

Dice: To cut food into small cubes that are the same size and shape

Garnish: To decorate a finished dish, usually with lemon wedges, parsley, or other herbs

Grill: To cook over intense heat

Pare: To peel or trim vegetables

Pit: To take out the center seed of a fruit

Roast: To cook in an oven

Roux: A mixture of flour and oil, fat, or butter used to thicken soups, stews, and sauces

Sauté: To cook food quickly in a small amount of oil

Sear: To quickly brown the outside of meats at a high temperature

The Great Escape!

Harry Houdini is one of the most famous magicians in history. He was known to escape from any handcuffs, chains, or jail cells that he encountered. One of his most famous acts was The Vanishing Elephant. This was a trick he performed in New York City in 1918.

NOW YOU SEE IT!
NOW YOU DON'T!

Fill in the shapes that contain a dot to reveal the hidden picture from Houdini's past.

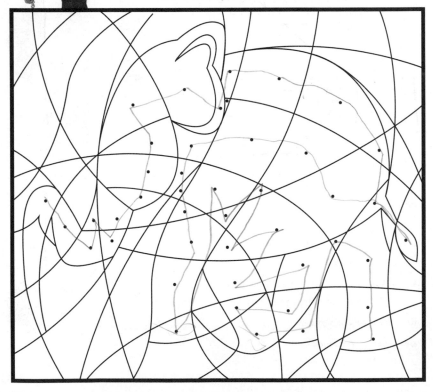

Selfies with Andy

Andy Warhol was the founder of the Pop Art movement. He loved to go to parties and photograph his friends. If he were alive today, he would most definitely be a fan of the selfie.

Draw selfies of you and your friends next to Andy.

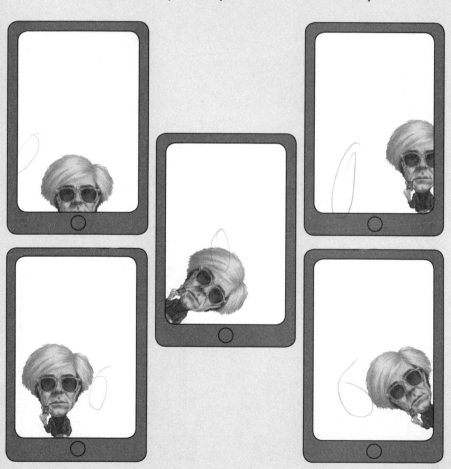

POTUS

The president of the United States (or POTUS) has to look sharp when appearing in public and making speeches. Design each president's necktie.

Battle of the Lees

Test your knowledge of three of the most famous "Lees" in history: comic-book creator Stan Lee, martial artist and movie star Bruce Lee, and Civil War leader Robert E. Lee.

Draw a line between each fact and its matching Lee.

Robert E. Lee

- Studying philosophy in college taught me that being prepared is the best way to avoid a fight, not start one.

- Robert Louis Stevenson's *The Strange Case of Dr. Jekyll and Mr. Hyde* inspired one of my most popular characters.

- I was so strong, I could do fifty chin-ups with only one arm.

- I became a soldier because my family did not have enough money to send me to college.

- I created a shy, nerdy superhero who was unlike all the other giant, muscle-bound heroes in other comic books.

- I helped redraw maps to include land won by the United States during the Mexican-American War.

- My motto is "Excelsior!"

- I said I would rather "die a thousand deaths" than surrender.

- I was born in 1940, in the year and the hour of the dragon.

- I was accused of committing treason.

- I changed the company name of Timely Comics to Marvel Comics.

- I once said, "If the enemy is cool, stay cooler than him. If the enemy moves, move faster than him."

Stan Lee

Bruce Lee

Two Truths and a Lie

Did you know that the famous story of George Washington cutting down a cherry tree was actually made up?

Look at the sentences below, and circle which one in each group of three is a lie about the father of our country.

- I wore false teeth made of wood.
- People considered calling me "His Elective Highness" or "His Mightiness," but I said "Mr. President" would do fine.
- In the 1750s, I wrote a journal about my travels that was published in newspapers, and it made me famous.

- My first job was as a surveyor (someone who measures and marks property boundaries).
- My French and German advisers helped me and my troops win our war against the British.
- I was the second president of the United States.

I CANNOT TELL A LIE.

- The French joined with my army to help us fight the British.
- No building in Washington, DC, is taller than the monument that was built to honor me.
- I won every battle I fought as commander of the Continental Army.

Famous Brain

Albert Einstein was one of the greatest scientific minds in history. He began writing scientific essays when he was only a teenager and had his first paper published when he was twenty-two. He became a world-famous scientist. One interesting fact about him was that his brain weighed less than the average human brain.

Solve this maze for the other half of Einstein's famous equation connecting mass and energy. What does *E* equal?

START!

E

MC^2

FINISH!

IMAGINATION IS MORE IMPORTANT THAN KNOWLEDGE.

Apple Picking

Johnny Appleseed is one of the great heroes of American folklore. Here are some real facts about this larger-than-life hero.

Connect the apple seeds to finish the picture.

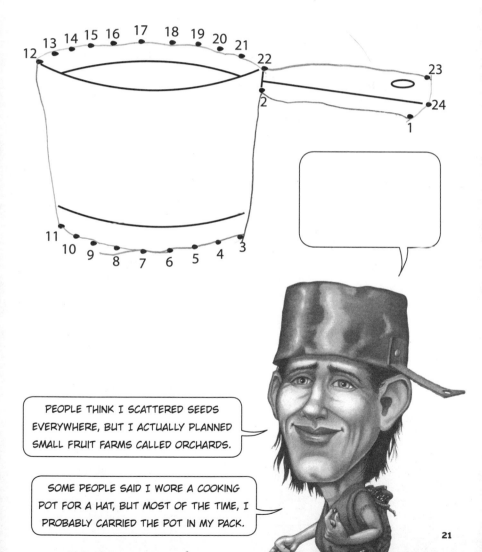

PEOPLE THINK I SCATTERED SEEDS EVERYWHERE, BUT I ACTUALLY PLANNED SMALL FRUIT FARMS CALLED ORCHARDS.

SOME PEOPLE SAID I WORE A COOKING POT FOR A HAT, BUT MOST OF THE TIME, I PROBABLY CARRIED THE POT IN MY PACK.

Carve Your Own Mount Rushmore

The Mount Rushmore National Memorial in South Dakota features four prominent presidents of the United States carved into the rock face of the mountain.

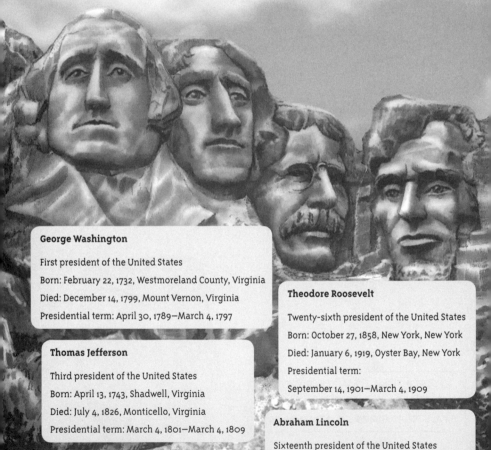

George Washington

First president of the United States

Born: February 22, 1732, Westmoreland County, Virginia

Died: December 14, 1799, Mount Vernon, Virginia

Presidential term: April 30, 1789–March 4, 1797

Thomas Jefferson

Third president of the United States

Born: April 13, 1743, Shadwell, Virginia

Died: July 4, 1826, Monticello, Virginia

Presidential term: March 4, 1801–March 4, 1809

Theodore Roosevelt

Twenty-sixth president of the United States

Born: October 27, 1858, New York, New York

Died: January 6, 1919, Oyster Bay, New York

Presidential term:
September 14, 1901–March 4, 1909

Abraham Lincoln

Sixteenth president of the United States

Born: February 12, 1809, Hodgenville, Kentucky

Died: April 15, 1865, Washington, DC

Presidential term: March 4, 1861–April 15, 1865

Draw yourself and your friends on your own version of Mount Rushmore.

The Odditorium

Believe It or Not: Robert Ripley was also known as the world's most traveled man. And he once had a job polishing tombstones. No wonder he was drawn to the wacky and the weird!

Ripley sold an illustration to *Life* magazine when he was still in high school. He went on to draw cartoons for the *New York Globe* in every section of the newspaper.

He created a weekly newspaper column called *Believe It or Not!* He drew the oddities and the amazing records set by the people he encountered on his world travels.

Look at the two illustrations below, and circle the differences in Ripley's collection of odd objects.

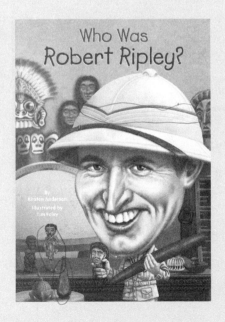 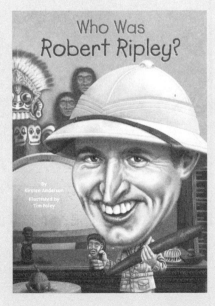

Also Known As

Many famous people in history aren't known by their birth names! Check out the real names of some of history's greatest movers and shakers, and then draw a line matching each real name to the more famous name.

Real Name	Famous Name
Samuel Clemens	Mother Teresa
Cassius Clay Jr.	Stan Lee
Erik Weisz	Mark Twain
Rolihlahla Mandela	Johnny Appleseed
Andrew Warhola	Andy Warhol
Agnes Bojaxhiu	Harry Houdini
John Chapman	Dr. Seuss
Theodor Geisel	Muhammad Ali
Stanley Lieber	Nelson Mandela

If you could go by another name, what would you like to be aka (also known as)?

_____

_____

_____

Build Your Own Town

Milton Hershey left school when he was around twelve years old and started working at an ice-cream parlor, the perfect job for a boy who would go on to build the world's biggest chocolate company. He opened his first candy shop when he was nineteen years old. By 1904, he had invented a formula for milk chocolate that could be molded into bars.

Milton built a large chocolate factory and a town around the factory for the workers to live in. The town had everything a person would need: a post office, a bank, theaters, parks, and even a zoo! The main intersection in the town of Hershey, Pennsylvania, is Cocoa Avenue and Chocolate Avenue.

Use this space to draw your perfect town.
Map out the streets, houses, and other important buildings
and spaces. Be sure to include what's important—
maybe even a chocolate factory of your own.

What Is a King without a Sandwich?

How did the man who developed the peanut plant in the United States influence the King of Rock and Roll?

George Washington Carver was born a slave in Missouri in the 1860s. After the Civil War, he became the first black student at Iowa State Agricultural College, where he studied botany. He went on to become the school's first black faculty member.

Much of his work centered around peanuts. In 1921, he spoke to Congress about the importance of the peanut plant and became known for his work with it. While he didn't invent peanut butter, his recipes using peanuts certainly popularized the food. Some of his experiments with peanuts led to the creation of peanut soaps, shaving cream, and shampoos!

Several decades later, Elvis Presley became known for his singing voice, his swinging hips, and his love of peanut-butter-and-banana sandwiches.

Try Elvis Presley's favorite sandwich!

INGREDIENTS

2 tablespoons peanut butter (preferably smooth)

2 slices white sandwich bread

1 small ripe banana, mashed with a fork (about 1/4 cup)

2 tablespoons butter

ASSEMBLY

***Be sure to ask an adult for help!**

1. Spread peanut butter evenly on 1 slice of bread, then spread mashed banana on other slice. Close sandwich, gently pressing bread slices together.

2. Heat butter in a skillet until melted.

3. Fry sandwich in the skillet until golden brown, turning over once, about 2 minutes total. Enjoy!

What is your favorite sandwich?

Pile it up—or write out the recipe—on this piece of bread.

Avocado cut
bread
salt
Pepper
toaster

Braille Decoder

Louis Braille went blind as a three-year-old, and by the time he was fifteen, he had created a code of raised dots to allow other blind people to read. Before Braille invented his code, blind people read books that had raised letters for the readers to touch. Many of those books were so thick, they weighed close to ten pounds!

The Braille Alphabet

A	B	C	D	E	F
G	H	I	J	K	L
M	N	O	P	Q	R
S	T	U	V	W	X
Y	Z				

[handwritten at top:] HeoPenedTheDoorsof KnowLEdge

Using the Braille alphabet, decode the message that appears on a plaque outside Louis Braille's childhood home.

⠓⠑ ⠕⠏⠑⠝⠑⠙ ⠞⠓⠑ ⠙⠕⠕⠗⠎ ⠕⠋ ⠅⠝⠕� ⠇⠑⠙⠛⠑

[handwritten on line:] He opened the Doors of Knowl Edge

⠠⠊ ⠇⠑⠁⠗⠝⠑⠙ ⠞⠓⠑ ⠺⠕⠗⠙ ⠺⠁⠞⠑⠗

I LEARNED HOW TO READ USING LOUIS BRAILLE'S CODE.

Helen Keller

Scientists and Inventors

We owe a great big "thanks" to the scientists and inventors described below. Their discoveries and inventions have changed the course of history over many centuries. Answer the questions, and test your knowledge.

Across

5. A cofounder of Apple. Without him, the Macintosh computer and the iPhone would not exist.

6. This woman was awarded the Nobel Prize twice and discovered radium.

7. A cofounder of Microsoft, who dropped out of Harvard to start his own company

8. One of the inventors of calculus, who named the force of gravity

Down

1. The inventor of the telephone, who taught at a school for the deaf in Boston

2. In addition to developing the first practical lightbulb, this inventor also created the phonograph (a machine that can record sound and then play it back again).

3. The father of modern science, who was the first to use the telescope for astronomy and helped prove that the earth revolves around the sun

4. A Founding Father, who was present at the signing of the Declaration of Independence and is known for flying a kite in a lightning storm

Alexander Graham Bell   Thomas Edison
Benjamin Franklin   Galileo
                         Steve Jobs
                         Marie Curie
                         Bill Gates
                         Isaac Newton

33

Chasing Rabbits

Beatrix Potter is best known for writing *The Tale of Peter Rabbit*, a book about a young rabbit and his adventures in the English countryside. Potter's interest in the natural world around her led her to sketch small animals, fossils, and fungi (mushrooms) for fun.

How many bunnies, mushrooms, and fossils can you fit onto Beatrix's hat?

Silly Words

Many storytellers of the past invented words that we use today! The examples below are the first known appearances of these words in print.

In William Shakespeare's plays, you can find words that he created, like *assassination*, *bedazzled*, and *zany*.

Charles Dickens first coined the words *boredom* and *flummox* in his books.

Thank you, Mark Twain, for *hard-boiled*.

J. R. R. Tolkien invented the word *tween* in his novel *The Lord of the Rings*, but when he used it, the word described a person in their twenties.

NERD!

Edgar Allan Poe was one of the first to use the word *tintinnabulation*, which means a ringing or tinkling sound.

Dr. Seuss even invented the word *nerd*!

Make up your own words and write their definitions on the lines below.

_____

_____

_____

_____

_____

_____

Theme-Park Builder

Walt Disney got his start drawing advertisements in newspapers and magazines, and went on to lead one of the largest animation companies in the world. He retold the stories of Snow White, Cinderella, Sleeping Beauty, and many, many more fairy-tale characters.

Walt wasn't limited to making films, though. One of his most famous achievements is his theme park, Disneyland. After the success of Disneyland, his company went on to build successful parks across the world in Orlando, Florida; Tokyo, Japan; Paris, France; and Hong Kong and Shanghai, China.

I THINK EVERY PARK NEEDS A CASTLE!

Now it's your turn to build your dream theme park.
Walt's Disneyland was inspired by stories of the Western
frontier, pirates, princesses, and the future.
What inspires your park?
What kind of rides would you include?
Don't forget to add your mascot!

What's Your Set List?

Reginald Kenneth Dwight started playing the piano when he was only three years old. He grew up to become one of the biggest pop stars of all time: Elton John!

As a teen, Elton began to focus on rock and roll, and to leave his training in classical music behind.

He released his first album in 1969 and has remained popular ever since with songs like "Your Song," "Tiny Dancer," and "Crocodile Rock." He is known for his outrageous stage costumes, boots, and glasses. Elton is still writing music and performing today.

It's always important for a musician to have a set list of the songs they will perform during each show. Make a set list of your favorite songs to sing on the lines below.

A Bright Idea!

Thomas Edison changed the world when he invented the first practical lightbulb and brought electricity into the mainstream. When he was testing his lightbulb, he used many interesting materials, including bamboo, spiderwebs, and even human hair. After he had success with the lightbulb, he built power plants to spread electricity across the country.

He also built the first motion-picture studio in America, called the Black Maria, in 1893.

Edison invented the phonograph—a machine for recording and playing back sound.

Without Edison, we wouldn't have many of the things we use every day. **Connect the dots to reveal one of Edison's most famous inventions.**

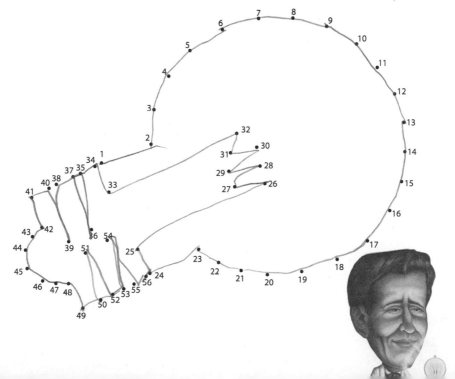

Girl Power!

Learn more about some of America's famous women in this word search.

Abigail Adams was the first first lady to live in the White House. She was such a close adviser to her husband while he was president that some people called her "Mrs. President." Unlike many people in her time, she believed strongly in equal rights for women and the abolition of slavery.

G	I	D	O	C	S	A	X	R	M	K	E	Z	P	D	E
B	L	R	F	P	G	B	K	C	E	F	L	B	G	F	B
N	Q	U	I	A	Z	I	O	L	B	W	E	I	L	H	G
W	Y	T	J	S	U	G	A	M	R	Q	A	U	O	A	U
S	U	S	A	N	B	A	N	T	H	O	N	Y	R	L	F
P	K	I	I	M	H	I	X	Q	E	B	O	F	I	Q	X
A	M	A	B	O	E	L	L	E	H	C	I	M	A	W	O
N	I	Z	E	T	L	A	N	A	Y	T	M	V	S	I	S
J	A	H	G	E	A	D	E	B	J	W	G	B	T	Q	K
O	G	S	E	H	T	A	T	P	O	U	U	N	E	W	A
B	E	T	Y	A	K	M	O	U	T	H	Y	T	I	A	L
S	O	V	L	V	E	S	H	O	U	T	D	S	N	P	Z
E	L	E	A	N	O	R	R	O	O	S	E	V	E	L	T
L	W	I	U	R	F	Z	P	Y	T	E	J	R	M	A	Y

Abigail Adams **Michelle Obama**

Eleanor Roosevelt **Gloria Steinem** **Susan B. Anthony**

Susan B. Anthony was from a Quaker family. She and her sisters were educated along with her brothers. She believed that women should have the right to vote. The first volume of the book she cowrote about the fight for women's rights was published in 1881. She campaigned for women's right to vote, but died before it was added to the Constitution as the Nineteenth Amendment.

Eleanor Roosevelt was the first first lady to hold press conferences about the issues of the day. She was the first lady of the United States longer than anyone else and took on the nickname of "the First Lady of the World." She helped start the United Nations, and President Truman chose her as a representative for the United States.

Gloria Steinem is known as a champion of women's rights. She has always spoken out about the unfair treatment of women. Early in her career, she struggled to find a serious writing job, because women were expected to write only about fashion and beauty. In 1970, she spoke in front of the US Senate in support of the Equal Rights Amendment.

Michelle Obama was the first African American first lady of the United States. She skipped the second grade and started taking college courses in sixth grade. She was Barack Obama's mentor at the law firm where they worked. After moving into the White House with her two daughters, she was sometimes known as "mom in chief."

Action!

Movie directors are the geniuses who help create your favorite films. They work with actors, producers, writers, editors, and many other behind-the-scenes people to make great movies.

A storyboard helps the director know how to organize the scenes in a movie. Draw a storyboard for your own epic feature film!

1

2

3

4

WE WORKED TOGETHER TO CREATE THE INDIANA JONES MOVIES!

George Lucas

Steven Spielberg

5

6

7

8

9

BOO!

I AM KNOWN AS A MASTER OF SUSPENSE FILMS.

Alfred Hitchcock

Beatlemania

John Lennon, Paul McCartney, George Harrison, and Ringo Starr came to America in the early 1960s and started what was called "the British Invasion." Their mop-top hairstyles and catchy music took the country by storm. They soon became some of the biggest stars in the world.

Help! the Beatles go on their world tour, and discover facts about the Fab Four along the way!

FACT: One of their first gigs was in a seedy little club in Germany.

FACT: Their first hit was a song called "Please Please Me."

FACT: Their music had the "Mersey Sound," named after a river that runs through their hometown of Liverpool, England.

FACT: The Beatles arrived in America on February 7, 1964.

FACT: In addition to being rock stars, the Beatles also starred in movies like *A Hard Day's Night* and *Help!*

Mapping the World

Without the discoveries of these brave explorers, the world would be a much smaller place.

Answer the questions, and test your knowledge about the people who helped fill in the blank spots on the map.

Across

1. On his first voyage to the New World, he sailed with three ships: the *Niña*, the *Pinta*, and the *Santa María*.

7. The very first person to step foot on the moon, this explorer earned his pilot's license before earning his driver's license.

Down

2. This young woman joined the Lewis and Clark expedition because they needed someone who could speak the Shoshone language.

3. One of the most well-known Antarctic explorers in history, he was the first man to take aerial photos of Antarctica from a hot-air balloon.

4. This pilot was the first woman to fly solo across the Atlantic Ocean in 1932.

5. This sailor's journey proved that the earth was round. He also named the Pacific Ocean.

6. Born in 1254 in Venice, Italy, he is known for traveling to Asia from Europe. It took him three and a half years to travel back to Italy from China.

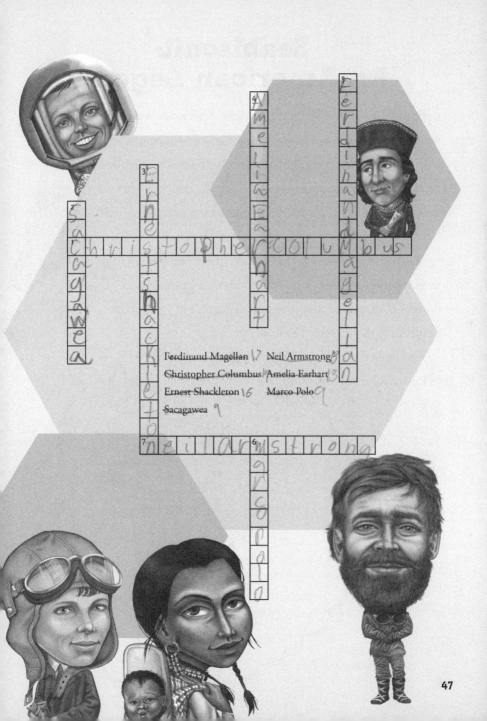

Ferdinand Magellan
Christopher Columbus
Ernest Shackleton
Sacagawea
Neil Armstrong
Amelia Earhart
Marco Polo

Seabiscuit:
An American Legend

Born in 1933 on a farm in Kentucky, Seabiscuit was a young horse that was bred for racing, but he was kind of lazy. He liked to sleep a lot and eat a lot. Working with the right trainer, he began to win horse races and beat some of the best horses in the country. He was voted Horse of the Year in 1938 and has stayed in America's hearts for decades.

When a horse wins a major race, there are many ways to celebrate their win. Many times, a garland of flowers is draped around the horse's neck. Fill in the beautiful garland around Seabiscuit's neck.

The horses and their jockeys are also given trophies to honor their success.

What are you the best at? What do you dream of succeeding at?
Create your own trophies to celebrate your successes below.

Artistic Friends

Two great twentieth-century artists, Frida Kahlo and Pablo Picasso, became friends when Frida visited Paris in 1939.

Many of Frida Kahlo's paintings depicted images of Mexican history and culture.

**Draw a mural below showing a scene from
your personal history or culture.**

Both Frida Kahlo and Pablo Picasso were known for painting self-portraits. How do you see yourself? Draw your self-portrait below!

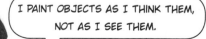

I PAINT OBJECTS AS I THINK THEM, NOT AS I SEE THEM.

I PAINT MYSELF BECAUSE I AM SO OFTEN ALONE AND BECAUSE I AM THE SUBJECT I KNOW BEST.

Batter Up!

Many famous baseball players broke records and barriers, hitting home runs into history.

No one expected a young boy from Puerto Rico, like Roberto Clemente, to make it big. He became an all-star, MVP, and twelve-time Gold Glove winner.

I WAS THE FIRST AFRICAN AMERICAN TO PLAY MAJOR LEAGUE BASEBALL.

Jackie Robinson

Babe Ruth

I WAS KNOWN AS THE HOME RUN KING!

Roberto Clemente

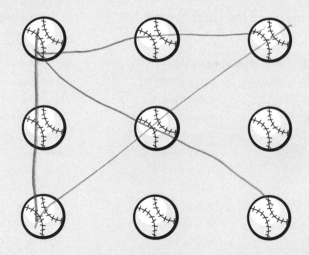

What's Your Pirate Name?

The legend of Blackbeard has influenced pirate lore for over three hundred years. After most likely starting his career as a British sailor during Queen Anne's War, Blackbeard soon moved to the Bahamas, where he was taught how to go "a-pirating" by Captain Benjamin Hornigold. After taking command of his own ship, Blackbeard began stealing other people's ships in the Caribbean and along the Eastern Seaboard of the United States.

Blackbeard got his pirate name because of his thick black beard. Make your own pirate name using the chart below!

The first letter of your first name		Month you were born
A: Scallywag	**N:** Sharp-Toothed	**January:** Magee
B: Peg-Leg	**O:** One-Eyed	**February:** Bartleby
C: Scurvy Dog	**P:** Greedy	**March:** the Mad
D: Captain	**Q:** Stinky Bob	**April:** Sparrow
E: The Fearsome	**R:** Two-Toed	**May:** Joe
F: Villainous	**S:** Jaundiced	**June:** Toe Jam
G: Mad	**T:** Jolly	**July:** of the Ocean
H: Evil	**U:** Dead Man	**August:** the Rapscallion
I: Bleeding Gums	**V:** Fire-Breathing Jim	**September:** the Smelly
J: Skull-Faced	**W:** Cold Sam	**October:** Spike
K: Toothless	**X:** Squidlegs	**November:** the Bloody
L: Salty	**Y:** Seastrong	**December:** Smee
M: Dead-Eye	**Z:** Rat-Face	

Shipshape!

When it comes to exploring the world, history is filled with interesting ship names.

Ernest Shackleton had two ships that he sailed while traveling to Antarctica: the *Endurance* and the *Nimrod*.

When Charles Darwin traveled around the world, he sailed in a ship called the *Beagle*.

When Ferdinand Magellan set out to circumnavigate the world, his ship was the *Trinidad*.

You can name your ship after a person. Or you can name your ship after a place or something you like very much. Name your ship!

BB Ship

Ferdinand Magellan

Charles Darwin

POEtry

Edgar Allan Poe was born in Boston in 1809 and orphaned at age two. He was soon adopted by a Virginian merchant family who sold, among other things, tombstones! Is it a surprise that he became known for writing such dark and gloomy stories?

His poem *The Raven* was a huge success. He is considered to be the inventor of detective fiction and the father of American mystery writing.

Try writing some poems of your own! A limerick has five lines. Each line should have a certain number of syllables (9-9-6-6-9). The last word of lines one, two, and five should rhyme, and so should the last word of lines three and four.

Here's a spooky example:

There once was a very old specter

who loved to eat apricot nectar.

So he haunted the trees

to scare off hungry bees,

and now he's a nectar collector.

Write your own limerick on the lines below!

Haikus are easier. They're only three lines long, no rhyming needed! Each haiku follows a syllable pattern of 5-7-5.

Here's a Who Was? example:

Read biographies.

Learn facts, gain inspiration,

and get good grades, too.

Write your haiku below!

_____

_____

_____

Great Artists

Learn more about some of history's greatest visual artists in this word search.

I	F	T	H	M	X	P	D	Y	G	I	I	X	J	Z
T	C	R	P	Z	O	I	P	E	I	L	H	L	B	K
G	Y	N	I	A	A	Y	X	H	O	N	O	O	A	W
E	O	P	I	Z	B	A	G	H	G	L	K	N	A	K
W	D	W	O	V	F	L	R	R	A	I	U	C	T	J
B	P	O	N	C	A	A	O	V	J	S	I	E	Z	X
Y	O	F	P	U	W	D	V	P	B	Z	N	K	W	V
C	O	S	C	Y	A	C	O	O	I	O	K	J	P	I
K	P	Z	D	A	U	M	T	D	M	C	D	K	L	I
S	K	N	L	X	Y	H	C	E	R	V	A	D	P	E
N	A	I	B	I	C	N	D	B	Y	A	U	S	G	C
U	A	G	M	Z	A	U	C	G	F	Q	N	Y	S	S
O	L	H	A	K	A	D	I	R	F	D	P	O	N	O
Q	L	I	B	L	X	P	T	Y	X	A	Y	E	E	P
W	I	T	C	U	T	I	S	Q	G	C	E	J	E	L

Andy Warhol

Frida Kahlo

Pablo Picasso

Claude Monet

Leonardo da Vinci

Andy Warhol was known for creating Pop Art using images of celebrities like Marilyn Monroe and Elvis Presley. He believed art could be about fun, cheap things, as well as serious, important things. He could often be seen wearing a silver wig and sunglasses.

Frida Kahlo was one of the most famous female artists of all time. Her real first name was Magdalena. Many of her paintings included religious symbols and images from Mexican folk art. One of her most famous paintings is called *What the Water Gave Me*.

Pablo Picasso started selling his art when he was nine years old, and he had his first art show when he was thirteen. Not one to stick with the same old style, he would try out new and different ideas as soon as he felt he had mastered one particular style of art. One critic described his painting as "the work of a madman."

Leonardo da Vinci lived in Florence, Italy, in the 1400s. In addition to being a painter, he was an inventor, an engineer, a scientist, and a musician. His notebooks full of ideas and drawings are considered treasures today. His most famous painting is the *Mona Lisa*.

Claude Monet was a French painter known for working in a style called Impressionism. He believed that people should paint what they actually saw, rather than trying to make things look perfect. In addition to being a famous painter, he was quite well known for being a gardener. One of his most famous paintings is *Water Lilies*.

Bill and Steve's Excellent Adventure

Bill Gates and Steve Jobs were two of the most successful computer innovators of the twentieth century. Compare the two computer rivals below, and connect each fact to the correct tech genius.

- My parents adopted me in 1955.
- I wrote my first computer program when I was thirteen years old.
- I loved to eat fruit, so I named my company after my favorite fruit of all, the apple!
- I created the software known as Windows.
- A famous commercial for my company aired during the Super Bowl in 1984.
- I got an honorary degree from Harvard University, after quitting more than thirty years earlier!
- I was a driving force in computer animation and convinced Disney to pay Pixar to make three full-length animated films.
- I started teaching myself computer languages in seventh grade.
- I became a millionaire when I was twenty-five years old.
- I became a self-made billionaire when I was thirty-one years old.

Bill Gates

Steve Jobs

60

Maria Tallchief: Osage Ballerina

Maria Tallchief was America's first prima ballerina, but her upbringing was not one that you would expect.

She was an American Indian who spent the early part of her childhood on an Osage reservation in Oklahoma. When she was eight years old, her family moved to California with hopes of Maria and her sister finding success in Hollywood. She started to take her dancing very seriously and realized that she wanted to be a ballerina.

She went on to become a member of the New York City Ballet and was even married to its artistic director and choreographer George Balanchine for a time. It was under his guidance that she became the country's first prima ballerina, dancing in many famous ballets, including *The Firebird*.

Decorate Maria's ballet slippers and her famous Firebird costume.

Stand Up for Your Rights

There have always been brave people willing to stand up for their rights and the rights of others.

Find the names of some of history's most well-known rights activists.

Across

5. Famous for not giving up her seat to a white passenger on a bus in Montgomery, Alabama, this woman was later called "the First Lady of civil rights" by the United States Congress.

 6. The first black president of South Africa, this man spent twenty-seven years in prison for challenging apartheid—segregation—in his country. His African name means "tree shaker."

7. This woman was a former slave who helped other slaves escape to freedom using the Underground Railroad. During the Civil War, she worked as both a nurse and a spy for the Union Army.

Down

 1. This female abolitionist and author fanned the flames that started the Civil War with the publication of her book *Uncle Tom's Cabin*.

2. This man was a former slave who started the civil rights movement. He secretly taught other slaves how to read and write, and helped recruit black soldiers to fight in the Union Army during the Civil War.

 3. A champion of independent India, this man walked 240 miles as part of a protest against the British. He believed that India should be governed by Indian citizens, not the British.

4. This civil rights champion led the March on Washington on August 28, 1963, and gave his famous "I Have a Dream" speech.

Frederick Douglass 17
Gandhi 6
Harriet Beecher Stowe 1a
Harriet Tubman 13
Martin Luther King Jr. 15
Nelson Mandela 13
Rosa Parks 8

Presidential Mix-Up!

Unscramble the presidents!

E O E R G G   A O N T W H G I N S

George Washington

M B A A R H A   L O I N C L N

Abraham Lincoln

H O N J   F .   D N E N K E Y

John F. Kennedy

R A N O L D   G A E R A N

Ranold Reagan

K A R A C B   M A A B O

Barack Obama

S A T H M O   F E F J E R S N O

Thomas Jefferson

R O O D E H T E   V T R O S O E E L

Theodore Roosvelt

K R A I N N L F   R T V O S O E L E

Franklin Roosevelt

O D O R O W W   S I L N O W

Woodrow Wilson

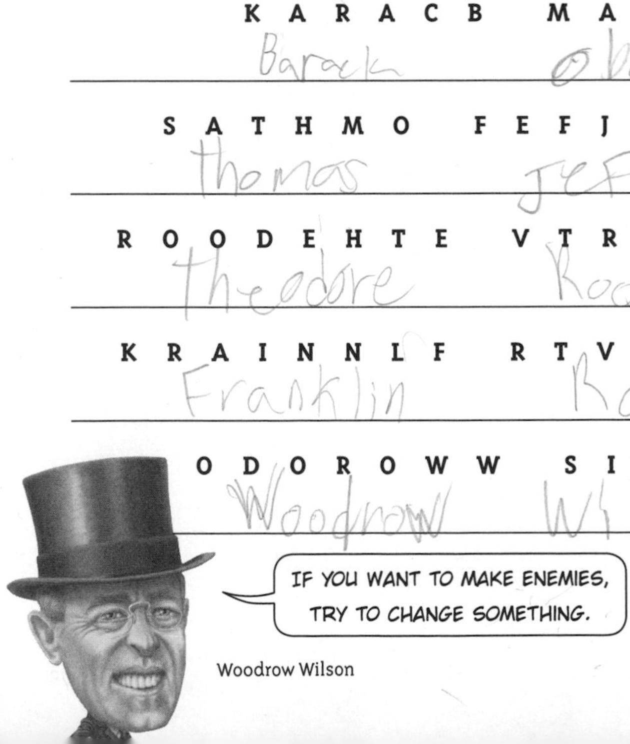

IF YOU WANT TO MAKE ENEMIES,
TRY TO CHANGE SOMETHING.

Woodrow Wilson

Fly Away!

Amelia Earhart first saw an airplane at the Iowa State Fair in 1908, when she was ten years old. She took her first ride in a plane when she was twenty-three years old, and within a year, she had earned her pilot's license.

In 1937, Amelia planned to become the first woman to fly all the way around the world. Sadly, during her attempt, she disappeared, and to this day, no one knows what happened to her.

Fill in the shapes that contain a dot to reveal Amelia's lifelong passion.

Keep Calm

Winston Churchill served as prime minister of the United Kingdom from 1940 to 1945 and again from 1951 to 1955. Widely regarded as one of the greatest wartime leaders of the twentieth century, Churchill was also a historian, a writer, and an artist.

He is the only British prime minister to have won the Nobel Prize in Literature and was the first person to be made an honorary citizen of the United States.

Like many historical figures, Winston Churchill is credited for saying something that he didn't actually say. While he might never have said "keep calm and carry on," the message is a strong one, and many people have given it their own meaning.

Fill in the blank for your own "Keep Calm" motto.

Flying Lesson

Orville and Wilbur Wright were high-school dropouts in Dayton, Ohio, who loved all things mechanical. They worked with printing presses, bicycles, and motors, all of which helped inspire their idea for the airplane. They studied the writings of other inventors to figure out how to build a flying machine.

Their first successful airplane flight was on December 17, 1903, in Kitty Hawk, North Carolina. Today, every single airplane includes at least one part that was created or refined by the Wright brothers.

You can make your own paper airplane and test it out just like the Wright brothers.

1. Get a sheet of paper.

2. Fold it in half lengthwise.

3. Fold the top corners in to the center. Make sure the folds are tight and crisp.

4. Fold the angled edges in to the center. Take the new angled sides and fold them both in to meet at the center line.

5. Fold along the center line. This fold should hide all the other folds inside.

6. Fold down the wings.

7. Take your airplane to the skies! Give it a toss and watch it fly!

Space: The Final Frontier

Humans have always dreamed of reaching the stars. Through programs like NASA, brave explorers have traveled vast distances in space.

Neil Armstrong was the first person to walk on the moon. Sally Ride was the first American woman in space.

Neil Armstrong

Sally Ride

MANY PEOPLE CALL ME THE FATHER OF MODERN SCIENCE. I DISCOVERED MANY MOONS OF THE PLANET JUPITER, INCLUDING THOSE LATER NAMED EUROPA, IO, GANYMEDE, AND CALLISTO.

Galileo

Help our astronauts navigate this outer-space maze.

With your pencil, draw a line through the galaxy.

Be careful not to touch the stars!

Musical Superstars

Get to know some of the biggest music superstars in history!

H	E	D	O	C	S	A	X	R	M	K	E	Z	P	D	E	T	A	C	Q	U
V	L	O	F	P	G	B	K	C	E	F	L	B	G	F	B	H	B	A	Z	R
N	Q	L	B	A	Z	I	O	L	B	W	E	I	B	H	G	E	O	U	I	Q
W	Y	L	O	U	I	S	A	R	M	S	T	R	O	N	G	B	J	N	B	Y
S	U	Y	J	N	B	A	N	T	H	O	N	Y	B	L	F	E	B	M	H	U
P	K	P	B	M	H	I	X	Q	E	B	O	F	D	Q	X	A	Y	O	E	K
A	M	A	Y	O	E	L	L	E	H	C	I	M	Y	W	O	T	I	T	L	M
N	I	R	I	T	L	A	N	A	Y	T	M	V	L	I	S	L	A	E	A	I
J	A	T	A	E	A	D	E	B	J	W	G	B	A	Q	K	E	N	H	T	A
O	G	O	N	H	T	A	T	P	O	U	U	N	N	W	A	S	Y	E	L	G
B	E	N	Y	E	L	V	I	S	P	R	E	S	L	E	Y	T	O	L	B	E
S	O	B	L	V	E	S	H	O	U	T	D	S	N	P	Z	R	A	R	M	O
E	L	U	A	B	O	R	R	N	O	S	E	V	W	L	T	P	N	T	H	L
W	O	L	F	G	A	N	G	A	M	A	D	E	U	S	M	O	Z	A	R	T

Dolly Parton   **Louis Armstrong**   **Elvis Presley**

The Beatles   **Bob Dylan**   **Wolfgang Amadeus Mozart**

Dolly Parton grew up in a large, poor family in Tennessee. She sang on the radio for the first time when she was only ten years old.

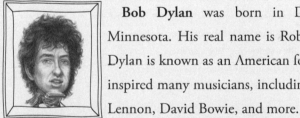

The Beatles were a British rock-and-roll band from Liverpool, England. John Lennon, Paul McCartney, George Harrison, and Ringo Starr became so popular that they couldn't go to restaurants or many public places!

Louis Armstrong grew up in New Orleans, Louisiana, in the early 1900s. By 1926, he was known as the world's greatest trumpet player.

Bob Dylan was born in Duluth, Minnesota. His real name is Robert Zimmerman. Bob Dylan is known as an American folk singer whose music inspired many musicians, including John Lennon, David Bowie, and more.

Elvis Presley was known as the King of Rock and Roll. His sound combined the blues, gospel music, and country-western-style classics into rock and roll.

Mozart was a classical composer who wrote more than six hundred concertos, sonatas, symphonies, and operas. He played the piano for the empress of Austria when he was only six years old.

On the Battlefield

The American Civil War, also known as the War Between the States, was fought from 1861 to 1865. It was a time of division in the United States. People in the North and the South disagreed over the expansion of slavery into new US territories.

Learn about some of the key players below, and then help Clara Barton get across the battlefield to find wounded soldiers.

Robert E. Lee

- Lee became a soldier because his family did not have enough money to send him to college.
- He graduated second in his class from the United States Military Academy at West Point.
- Abraham Lincoln requested that Lee lead troops for the Union Army, but he refused and became a valuable adviser to the president of the Confederate States of America.
- Lee said he would rather "die a thousand deaths" than surrender.
- He was defeated at the Battle of Gettysburg in Pennsylvania in July 1863.
- His surrender to General Grant signified the end of the Civil War.

Ulysses S. Grant

- Grant was a reluctant soldier who became a Civil War general.
- He didn't want to attend the United States Military Academy at West Point, but his father made him go.
- He commanded the Union Army at the Battle of Shiloh in Tennessee in April 1862.
- He famously told one of his enemies that he would only accept "unconditional and immediate surrender."
- One of his strategies for defeating the Confederacy was to capture and destroy their railroads.
- When General Lee's troops surrendered, Grant let the officers keep their horses and their personal weapons.
- After the Civil War ended, Grant was a war hero, and eventually he was elected the eighteenth president of the United States.

Clara Barton

- Clara Barton brought food and supplies that she paid for herself to soldiers fighting in the Civil War.
- She was a nurse during the war and was given the nickname "the angel of the battlefield" by an army surgeon.
- After the Civil War, she helped publish the names of Union soldiers who were missing or dead.
- She founded the American Red Cross.

Curse of the Mummy

King Tut is known as the "boy king" of Ancient Egypt. He died before he reached the age of twenty. In 1922, his tomb was discovered in the Valley of the Kings by Howard Carter. The discovery of Tut's tomb allowed a look into his history and death. His leg was broken when he died, and it's possible that an infection killed him.

Some people believe that Tut's tomb is cursed, because Lord Carnarvon, the man who paid for its excavation, died four months after the opening of the tomb.

Take a look at the two pictures of Tut and his tomb, and see if you spot any differences. Beware the curse!

Dear Diary

Anne Frank was a young Jewish girl who hid for nearly two years in the back-room office and warehouse of a building attached to her father's business before being found by the Nazis. When she celebrated her thirteenth birthday, she was given the diary that would survive after her death and bring her story to the world. She wrote about everything in her diary, from her crushes to the events of World War II. Her father found her diary and published it in 1947.

What kinds of things do you write in your diary?

DATE:

_____

_____

_____

_____

_____

_____

_____

_____

IN SPITE OF EVERYTHING I STILL BELIEVE THAT PEOPLE ARE REALLY GOOD AT HEART.

The Original Girl Guide

Sacagawea helped guide the Lewis and Clark expedition to the American Northwest. She set off with the expedition on April 7, 1805. She was originally recruited for her translation skills, but she proved to be an invaluable guide as well. The Lewis and Clark expedition used four languages: English, French, Minnetaree, and Shoshone.

In addition to guiding the expedition, she traveled nearly four thousand miles with her baby on her back.

Her travels with the Lewis and Clark expedition reunited her with her family, whom she had not seen for five years.

Lewis and Clark named a river in central Montana after her, to thank her for her help. Sacagawea has had more landmarks named for her and memorials built in her honor than any other American woman!

Help Sacagawea guide the Lewis and Clark expedition across the American Northwest to the Pacific Ocean.

I Am the Greatest!

Cassius Marcellus Clay Jr. was born in 1942 in Louisville, Kentucky. When he was twenty-two, he won the world heavyweight championship, joined the Nation of Islam, and changed his name to Muhammad Ali.

Muhammad Ali became a legend in the boxing world. He won the world heavyweight championship three times. Ali was well known for his unique boxing style, consisting of the Ali shuffle and the rope-a-dope.

Decorate your own championship belt.

FLOAT LIKE A BUTTERFLY, STING LIKE A BEE.

Driving with Henry Ford

Henry Ford was the clever engineer of the world's first mass-produced automobiles.

As a boy growing up on a farm in Michigan in the 1860s, Ford loved to take apart watches and wind-up toys, and then put them back together.

In 1879, he moved to Detroit, Michigan, to learn more about engines and manufacturing. After spending some time working with Thomas Edison, Henry Ford founded the Ford Motor Company, where he would invent and build cars.

Henry Ford believed that everyone should own a car because it gave them the freedom of travel.

What is your dream car? Draw it in the space below.

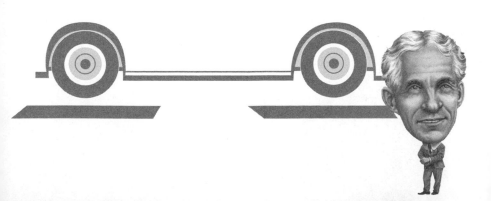

Follow the Underground Railroad

Harriet Tubman's father taught her how to move silently in the woods and how to find the North Star. That knowledge would be useful to her as she helped over three hundred slaves escape to freedom traveling the Underground Railroad.

The Underground Railroad was not a railroad with trains or tracks. But there were "conductors" who helped escaping slaves to freedom. Harriet Tubman was one of those conductors.

After Tubman escaped from slavery on her own, without her husband, parents, or brothers, the first slaves she helped escape were her sister and her sister's children. She also saved her parents and delivered them safely to Canada.

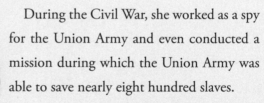

During the Civil War, she worked as a spy for the Union Army and even conducted a mission during which the Union Army was able to save nearly eight hundred slaves.

She was a powerful speaker who told her stories of narrow escapes and dangerous journeys on the Underground Railroad at antislavery meetings.

Help Harriet get to safety along the Underground Railroad.

Animal Lovers

These animal lovers have brought attention to animals around the world. Connect each animal lover to the correct facts.

I grew up on my parents' wildlife park in Australia.

When I was ten years old, I took a voyage across the Atlantic and fell in love with ships!

I grew up in England, and from a young age, I was fascinated by animal behavior.

I helped my father trap crocodiles when I was a child.

I was a pioneer of new techniques for diving, breathing, and filming underwater.

When I was twenty-six, I visited Africa and studied chimpanzees in their natural habitat.

I made scuba diving a popular, adventurous pastime in the 1950s.

I died when I was attacked by a stingray while filming a documentary.

I founded an institute in 1977 to raise awareness and understanding about the treatment of chimpanzees around the world.

Steve Irwin

Jacques Cousteau

Jane Goodall

The Fastest Man in the World

Born in rural Alabama, Jesse Owens suffered many hardships. As a boy he worked several jobs, like delivering groceries and working in a shoe-repair shop, to make ends meet.

He became a student athlete and ran track for Ohio State in college. In 1936, he competed in the Summer Olympics in Berlin, Germany. At the time, Berlin was under Nazi control, led by Adolf Hitler, so Jesse's presence as an African American brought attention to the racial issues at the Olympics that year. Jesse went on to win four gold medals in track and field. He became known as "the fastest man in the world."

Create your own gold medal!

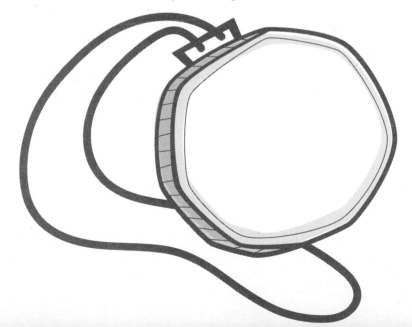

Make Your Own Comic

Stan Lee is known for his work with Marvel Comics and bringing Spider-Man and other superheroes to life. Beloved in the comic-book community, Stan Lee is responsible for some of the most famous comic-book characters, including the Fantastic Four, Daredevil, and Ant-Man. **Invent your own superhero, and create your own comic in the panels below.**

Count the Apples

Born on Christmas Day 1642, Isaac Newton was a secretive man who spent years trying to turn ordinary metals into gold. Although he failed in that pursuit, his other scientific research led him to discover and name the force of gravity. Some historians believe that he made his breakthrough discovery after an apple fell on his head. Ouch!

How many apples appear on these pages?

Watch Out for That Puck!

Wayne Gretzky is a Canadian hockey superstar. Nicknamed "the Great One" because he is considered to be the greatest hockey player of all time, Wayne played twenty seasons in the National Hockey League (NHL), and is the leading scorer in NHL history.

Help Wayne find these hockey-related terms in the word search below.

S	R	I	F	X	S	E	G	G	T	Y	B	S	S
E	I	D	I	K	P	N	I	A	T	P	A	C	Y
T	N	P	E	O	O	A	D	O	R	B	C	H	U
A	K	V	L	Q	R	P	H	F	W	U	P	T	J
K	G	O	A	L	T	C	U	J	P	O	N	P	Y
S	U	M	M	I	S	S	T	C	R	J	P	A	O
V	Y	X	D	N	M	B	I	T	K	G	J	L	M
J	A	K	M	D	A	N	N	S	P	S	Y	F	H
U	T	M	V	S	N	Z	I	X	S	M	O	E	T
V	N	J	Z	Y	S	G	I	C	P	A	Y	N	D
B	B	J	H	T	H	S	H	I	V	J	K	V	U
D	P	F	X	A	I	F	C	N	N	Q	D	F	V
G	Y	G	U	J	P	S	E	W	Y	K	P	I	E
Y	O	W	O	I	C	T	I	H	R	O	V	K	W

Goal	Trophy	Captain
Assist	Puck	Olympics
Skates	Rink	Sportsmanship
	Net	

Roosevelt on the Map

Theodore Roosevelt was the twenty-sixth president of the United States. He was also a cowboy, one of the leaders of the Rough Riders cavalry unit during the Spanish-American War, a hunter, and a naturalist—he loved the great outdoors!

Find these important places in Teddy Roosevelt's life in the word search below.

A	N	V	C	I	G	X	E	F	B	E	D	Y	Z	A
G	O	V	E	O	B	A	N	M	Y	I	J	F	M	T
F	D	C	D	H	W	I	O	K	L	R	K	A	Q	T
F	U	X	O	V	O	A	T	B	D	H	N	D	D	E
W	N	T	Y	F	K	G	S	X	I	A	Q	U	D	N
A	Y	S	S	U	O	R	W	H	P	Q	C	U	O	Q
D	T	A	T	E	B	Z	O	G	I	G	D	Y	D	T
I	D	K	E	N	D	L	L	Y	J	N	N	M	A	P
R	O	C	R	T	Z	A	L	F	W	A	G	H	Y	R
O	C	U	B	A	T	L	E	H	C	E	H	T	E	M
L	U	P	A	G	M	D	Y	D	M	D	N	S	O	D
F	P	O	Y	M	S	D	N	A	L	D	A	B	B	N
G	I	V	G	O	H	A	Z	A	M	Z	R	W	S	H
X	T	J	N	O	R	T	H	D	A	K	O	T	A	S
V	V	A	E	G	B	H	F	D	Z	O	U	S	R	O

New York	Cuba	Badlands
Panama	Yellowstone	Oyster Bay
Washington	Grand Canyon	North Dakota
	Florida	

Saint Joan

Joan of Arc was a French teenager. She saw visions. She spoke to angels. She wore her hair short and dressed like a boy.

And when her country needed her, she led an entire army into battle. In 1429, Joan was on a mission to save the town of Orléans from the English. She wore a suit of armor and carried her sword at her side. Joan carried a banner with angels on it. She raised her banner high as a symbol of hope for all of France.

Create your own banners with drawings and designs
that reflect your personal style.

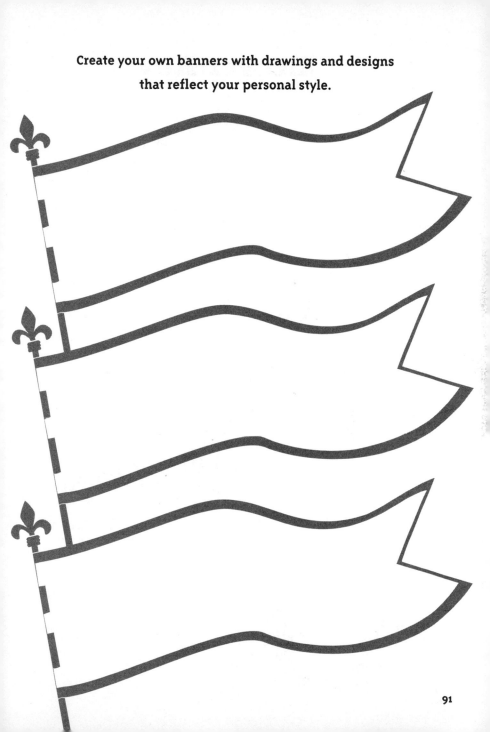

Answer Key

Pages 4–5

Across
5. Charles Dickens
8. Roald Dahl
9. Laura Ingalls Wilder

Down
1. William Shakespeare
2. Maurice Sendak
3. Mark Twain
4. J. K. Rowling
6. Edgar Allan Poe
7. Dr. Seuss

Page 7

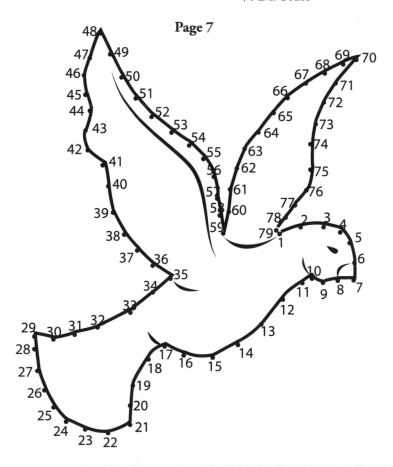

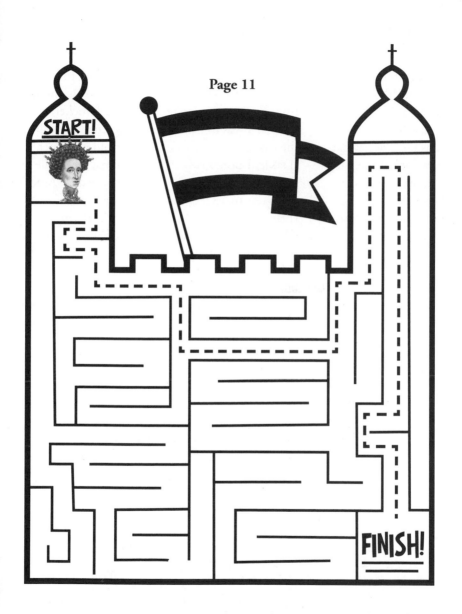

START!

FINISH!

Page 12

• I was born near what is now Birdsboro, Pennsylvania. (Daniel Boone)

• I was born near what is now Limestone, Tennessee. (Davy Crockett)

• I was known for my coonskin cap. (Davy Crockett)

• I was held captive by the American Indians from the Shawnee tribe because I was hunting on their lands. (Daniel Boone)

• I was elected to Congress in 1827. (Davy Crockett)

• As a teenager, I killed my first bear when I should have been tending my family's cows. (Daniel Boone)

• I claimed to have killed 105 bears in one season. (Davy Crockett)

• I rescued my thirteen-year-old daughter, Jemima, when she was kidnapped by American Indians. (Daniel Boone)

• I led the first pioneers across the Appalachian Mountains. (Daniel Boone)

• I fought and died at the Alamo. (Davy Crockett)

Page 13

H	S	I	N	R	A	G	A	R	M	E	H
A	A	V	F	O	G	G	R	R	E	F	A
D	U	Q	I	A	Z	O	O	L	B	W	B
B	T	Y	J	S	U	K	A	M	R	Q	R
S	E	W	D	X	J	V	S	A	Z	Y	O
E	K	I	I	M	P	I	T	Q	O	B	I
A	C	V	C	Y	E	N	G	R	I	L	L
R	X	Z	E	T	H	U	N	A	Y	T	M
S	A	H	G	P	A	R	E	B	J	W	G

• Studying philosophy in college taught me that being prepared is the best way to avoid a fight, not start one. (Bruce Lee)

• Robert Louis Stevenson's *The Strange Case of Dr. Jekyll and Mr. Hyde* inspired one of my most popular characters. (Stan Lee)

• I was so strong, I could do fifty chin-ups with only one arm. (Bruce Lee)

• I became a soldier because my family did not have enough money to send me to college. (Robert E. Lee)

• I created a shy, nerdy superhero who was unlike all the other giant, muscle-bound heroes in other comic books. (Stan Lee)

• I helped redraw maps to include land won by the United States during the Mexican-American War. (Robert E. Lee)

• My motto is "Excelsior!" (Stan Lee)

• I said I would rather "die a thousand deaths" than surrender. (Robert E. Lee)

• I was born in 1940, in the year and the hour of the dragon. (Bruce Lee)

• I was accused of committing treason. (Robert E. Lee)

• I changed the company name of Timely Comics to Marvel Comics. (Stan Lee)

• I once said, "If the enemy is cool, stay cooler than him. If the enemy moves, move faster than him." (Bruce Lee)

Page 19

• Lie: I wore false teeth made of wood.
• Lie: I was the second president of the United States.
• Lie: I won every battle I fought as commander of the Continental Army.

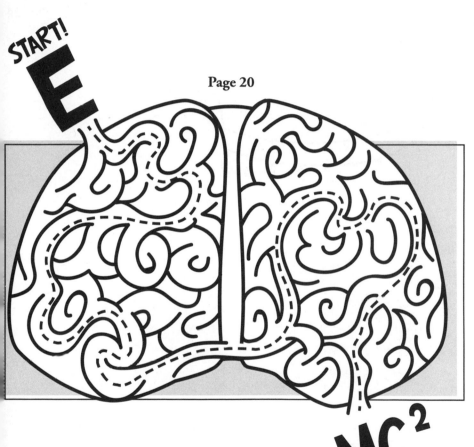

START!

E

MC²

FINISH!

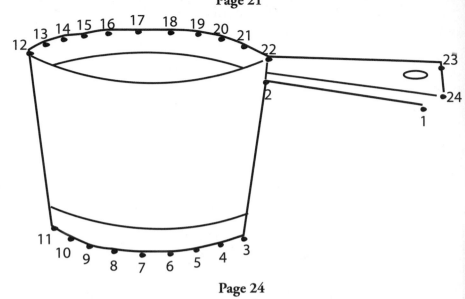

Page 24

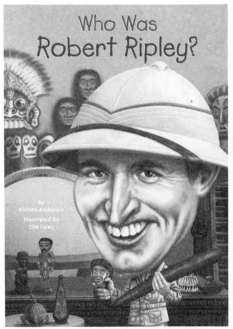
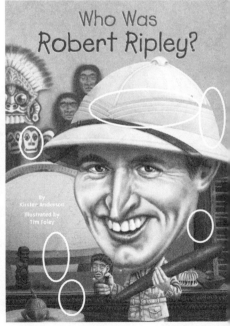

Page 25

Samuel Clemens—Mark Twain
Cassius Clay Jr.—Muhammad Ali
Erik Weisz—Harry Houdini
Rolihlahla Mandela—Nelson Mandela
Andrew Warhola—Andy Warhol
Agnes Bojaxhiu—Mother Teresa
John Chapman—Johnny Appleseed
Theodor Geisel—Dr. Seuss
Stanley Lieber—Stan Lee

Page 31

He opened the doors of knowledge to all
those who cannot see.

Pages 32–33

Across
5. Steve Jobs
6. Marie Curie
7. Bill Gates
8. Isaac Newton

Down
1. Alexander Graham Bell
2. Thomas Edison
3. Galileo
4. Benjamin Franklin

Page 39

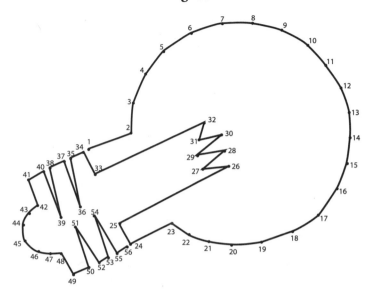

Pages 40–41

G	I	D	O	C	S	A	X	R	M	K	E	Z	P	D	E
B	L	R	F	P	G	B	K	C	E	F	L	B	G	F	B
N	Q	U	I	A	Z	I	O	L	B	W	E	I	L	H	G
W	Y	T	J	S	U	G	A	M	R	Q	A	U	O	A	U
S	U	S	A	N	B	A	N	T	H	O	N	Y	R	L	F
P	K	I	I	M	H	I	X	Q	E	B	O	F	I	Q	X
A	M	A	B	O	E	L	L	E	H	C	I	M	A	W	O
N	I	Z	E	T	L	A	N	A	Y	T	M	V	S	I	S
J	A	H	G	E	A	D	E	B	J	W	G	B	T	Q	K
O	G	S	E	H	T	A	T	P	O	U	U	N	E	W	A
B	E	T	Y	A	K	M	O	U	T	H	Y	T	I	A	L
S	O	V	L	V	E	S	H	O	U	T	D	S	N	P	Z
E	L	E	A	N	O	R	R	O	O	S	E	V	E	L	T
L	W	I	U	R	F	Z	P	Y	T	E	J	R	M	A	Y

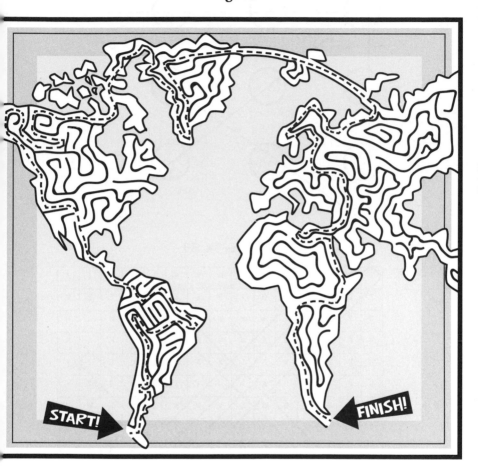

Pages 46–47

Across
1. Christopher Columbus
7. Neil Armstrong

Down
2. Sacagawea
3. Ernest Shackleton
4. Amelia Earhart
5. Ferdinand Magellan
6. Marco Polo

Page 53

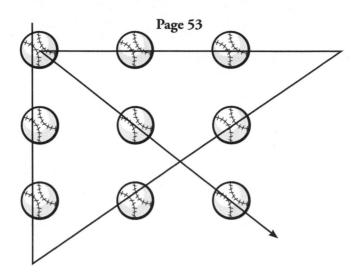

Pages 58–59

I	F	T	H	M	X	P	D	Y	G	I	I	X	J	Z
T	C	R	P	Z	O	I	P	E	I	L	H	L	B	K
G	Y	N	I	A	A	Y	X	H	O	N	O	O	A	W
E	O	P	I	Z	B	A	G	H	G	L	K	N	A	K
W	D	W	O	V	F	L	R	R	A	I	U	C	T	J
B	P	O	N	C	A	A	O	V	J	S	I	E	Z	X
Y	O	F	P	U	W	D	V	P	B	Z	N	K	W	V
C	O	S	C	Y	A	C	O	O	I	O	K	J	P	I
K	P	Z	D	A	U	M	T	D	M	C	D	K	L	I
S	K	N	L	X	Y	H	C	E	R	V	A	D	P	E
N	A	I	B	I	C	N	D	B	Y	A	U	S	G	C
U	A	G	M	Z	A	U	C	G	F	Q	N	Y	S	S
O	L	H	A	K	A	D	I	R	F	D	P	O	N	O
Q	L	I	B	L	X	P	T	Y	X	A	Y	E	E	P
W	I	T	C	U	T	I	S	Q	G	C	E	J	E	L

Page 60

- My parents adopted me in 1955. (Steve Jobs)
- I wrote my first computer program when I was thirteen years old. (Bill Gates)
- I loved to eat fruit, so I named my company after my favorite fruit of all, the apple! (Steve Jobs)
- I created the software known as Windows. (Bill Gates)
- A famous commercial for my company aired during the Super Bowl in 1984. (Steve Jobs)
- I got an honorary degree from Harvard University, after quitting more than thirty years earlier! (Bill Gates)
- I was a driving force in computer animation and convinced Disney to pay Pixar to make three full-length animated films. (Steve Jobs)
- I started teaching myself computer languages in seventh grade. (Bill Gates)
- I became a millionaire when I was twenty-five years old. (Steve Jobs)
- I became a self-made billionaire when I was thirty-one years old. (Bill Gates)

Pages 62–63

Across
5. Rosa Parks
6. Nelson Mandela
7. Harriet Tubman

Down
1. Harriet Beecher Stowe
2. Frederick Douglass
3. Gandhi
4. Martin Luther King Jr.

Page 64

EOERGG AONTWHGINS—George Washington
MBAARHA LOINCLN—Abraham Lincoln
HONJ F. DNENKEY—John F. Kennedy
RANOLD GAERAN—Ronald Reagan
KARACB MAABO—Barack Obama
SATHMO FEFJERSNO—Thomas Jefferson
ROODEHTE VTROSOEEL—Theodore Roosevelt
KRAINNLF RTVOSOELE—Franklin Roosevelt
ODOROWW SILNOW—Woodrow Wilson

Page 65

```
H E D O C S A X R M K E Z P D E T A C Q U
V L O F P G B K C E F L B G F B H B A Z R
N Q L B A Z I O L B W E I B H G E O U I Q
W Y L O U I S A R M S T R O N G B J N B Y
S U Y J N B A N T H O N Y B L F E B M H U
P K P B M H I X Q E B O F D Q X A Y O E K
A M A Y O E L L E H C I M Y W O T I T L M
N I R I T L A N A Y T M V L I S L A E A I
J A T A E A D E B J W G B A Q K E N H T A
O G O N H T A T P O U U N N W A S Y E L G
B E N Y E L V I S P R E S L E Y T O L B E
S O B L V E S H O U T D S N P Z R A R M O
E L U A B O R R N O S E V W L T P N T H L
W O L F G A N G A M A D E U S M O Z A R T
```

Page 73

Page 82

•I grew up on my parents' wildlife park in Australia. (Steve Irwin)

•When I was ten years old, I took a voyage across the Atlantic and fell in love with ships! (Jacques Cousteau)

•I grew up in England and from a young age, I was fascinated by animal behavior. (Jane Goodall)

•I helped my father trap crocodiles when I was a child. (Steve Irwin)

•I was a pioneer of new techniques for diving, breathing, and filming underwater. (Jacques Cousteau)

•When I was twenty-six, I visited Africa and studied chimpanzees in their natural habitat. (Jane Goodall)

•I made scuba diving a popular, adventurous pastime in the 1950s. (Jacques Cousteau)

•I died when I was attacked by a stingray while filming a documentary. (Steve Irwin)

•I founded an institute in 1977 to bring awareness and understanding about the treatment of chimpanzees around the world. (Jane Goodall)

Pages 86–87
69
(70 if you count the one Isaac is holding!)

S	R	I	F	X	S	E	G	G	T	Y	B	S	S
E	I	D	I	K	P	N	I	A	T	P	A	C	Y
T	N	P	E	O	O	A	D	O	R	B	C	H	U
A	K	V	L	Q	R	P	H	F	W	U	P	T	J
K	G	O	A	L	T	C	U	J	P	O	N	P	Y
S	U	M	M	I	S	S	T	C	R	J	P	A	O
V	Y	X	D	N	M	B	I	T	K	G	J	L	M
J	A	K	M	D	A	N	N	S	P	S	Y	F	H
U	T	M	V	S	N	Z	I	X	S	M	O	E	T
V	N	J	Z	Y	S	G	I	C	P	A	Y	N	D
B	B	J	H	T	H	S	H	I	V	J	K	V	U
D	P	F	X	A	I	F	C	N	N	Q	D	F	V
G	Y	G	U	J	P	S	E	W	Y	K	P	I	E
Y	O	W	O	I	C	T	I	H	R	O	V	K	W

Page 89

A	N	V	C	I	G	X	E	F	B	E	D	Y	Z	A
G	O	V	E	O	B	A	N	M	Y	I	J	F	M	T
F	D	C	D	H	W	I	O	K	L	R	K	A	Q	T
F	U	X	O	V	O	A	T	B	D	H	N	D	D	E
W	N	T	Y	F	K	G	S	X	I	A	Q	U	D	N
A	Y	S	S	U	O	R	W	H	P	Q	C	U	O	Q
D	T	A	T	E	B	Z	O	G	I	G	D	Y	D	T
I	D	K	E	N	D	L	L	Y	J	N	N	M	A	P
R	O	C	R	T	Z	A	L	F	W	A	G	H	Y	R
O	C	U	B	A	T	L	E	H	C	E	H	T	E	M
L	U	P	A	G	M	D	Y	D	M	D	N	S	O	D
F	P	O	Y	M	S	D	N	A	L	D	A	B	B	N
G	I	V	G	O	H	A	Z	A	M	Z	R	W	S	H
X	T	J	N	O	R	T	H	D	A	K	O	T	A	S
V	V	A	E	G	B	H	F	D	Z	O	U	S	R	O